THE WORLD AROUND YOU

UP, DOWN, AND AROUND THE CITY

by
Christianne Jones

PEBBLE
a capstone imprint

Published by Pebble, an imprint of Capstone
1710 Roe Crest Drive, North Mankato, Minnesota 56003
capstonepub.com

Library of Congress Cataloging-in-Publication Data
Names: Jones, Christianne C., author. Title: Up, down, and around the city / by Christianne
Jones. Description: North Mankato, Minnesota : Pebble, 2022. | Series: The world around
you | Audience: Ages 5-8 | Audience: Grades K-1 | Summary: "Zoom! The elevator zips
from the bottom floor to the top floor of a tall building. Beep! Beep! The subway stops
for people to get on and off. Using bright photographs and interactive, rhyming text, this
picture book will help young readers discover position words while exploring the city"
—Provided by publisher. Identifiers: LCCN 2021035305 (print) | LCCN 2021035306
(ebook) | ISBN 9781663976536 (hardcover) | ISBN 9781666326277 (paperback) | ISBN
9781666326284 (pdf) | ISBN 9781666326307 (kindle edition) Subjects: LCSH: Cities and
towns—Juvenile literature. Classification: LCC HT152 .J66 2022 (print) | LCC HT152
(ebook) | DDC 307.76—dc23 LC record available at https://lccn.loc.gov/2021035305
LC ebook record available at https://lccn.loc.gov/2021035306

Editorial Credits
Editor: Christianne Jones; Designer: Brann Garvey; Media Researcher: Svetlana Zhurkin;
Production Specialist: Laura Manthe

Image Credits
Getty Images: ziggy_mars, bottom left 28; Shutterstock: BluIz60, spread 14-15,
Cascade Creatives, spread 8-9, Dayah Shaltes, 19, EA Given, top left 28, Huy Thoai,
spread 16-17, imageportal, spread 22-23, Kenneth Sponsler, 10, Kseniia De Netto, bottom
right 29, lazyllama, spread 6-7, MikeDotta, top left 29, Monkey Business Images, top Cover,
Netrun78, middle right 28, pio3, 27, QQ7, spread 12-13, Rido, 11, Roschetzky Photography,
bottom Cover, Sara Kylee, 21, studioflara, 18, Sundry Photography, middle left 29,
unterwegs, 3, View Apart, spread 24-25, William Perugini, 26

Special thanks to Sveta Zhurkin and Dan Nunn for their consulting work and help.

POSITION WORDS ALL AROUND

Turn left. Turn right. Go up. Go down.

Position words help you get around town.

From the top of a skyscraper

everything looks pretty.

Position words are found all around the city!

PLENTIFUL POSITION WORDS

Position words are everywhere
describing where things are.
Let's visit city parks and streets
to find them near and far.

above/below

inside/outside

top/bottom

near/far

first/last

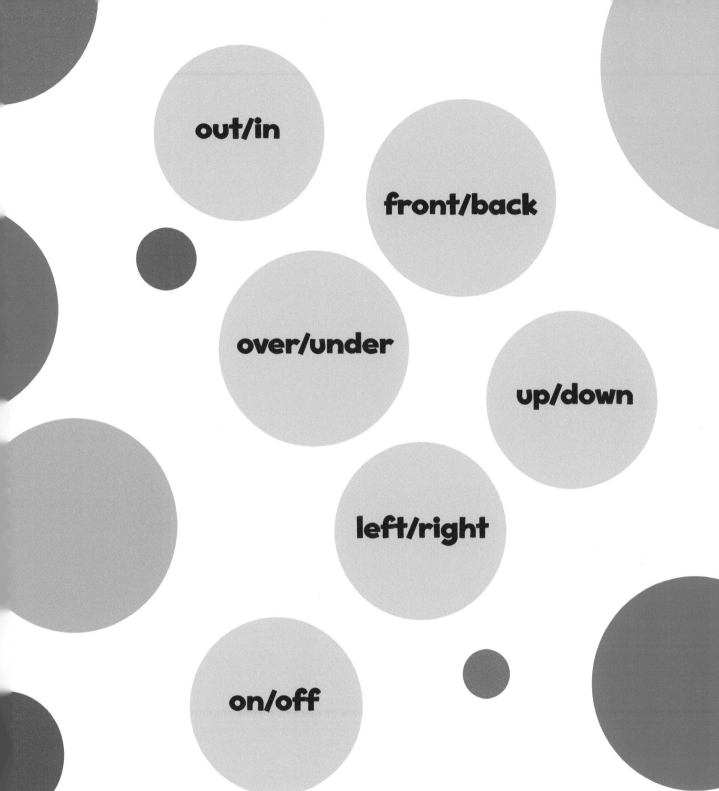

out/in

front/back

over/under

up/down

left/right

on/off

ABOVE/BELOW

A bridge **ABOVE** the river takes traffic to and fro, while a sightseeing boat glides quietly **BELOW**.

BOTTOM/TOP

At the **BOTTOM** of the ride
people wait in line.
At the **TOP** of the ride
people see the city shine.

OUTSIDE/INSIDE

Baked treats in the window
can be seen from **OUTSIDE**,

while **INSIDE** the head baker
beams with joy and pride.

A bench is **NEAR**. Take a break from your hike!

The buildings are **FAR**. You might need a bike.

LAST/FIRST

Being **LAST** in line takes patience at the food truck. Being **FIRST** in line takes timing and a little luck.

OUT/IN

The tunnel is busy with vehicles going **OUT** and **IN**.
If you don't get stuck in traffic, consider it a win!

FRONT/BACK

A summer concert in the park is a fun place to go.

It doesn't matter if you are in the **FRONT** or the **BACK** row.

OVER/UNDER

A rainbow arching **OVER** the city
puts on a colorful show,
making the buildings **UNDER** it
bask in a glorious glow.

At the subway station some people head **UP** to get into town, while others go the opposite way and head back **DOWN**.

LEFT/RIGHT

Getting through the city can cause lots of stress.
Do you go **LEFT** or **RIGHT**? Sometimes you guess.

OFF/ON

People **OFF** the subway play the waiting game,

while people **ON** the subway wait just the same.

WHERE IS IT QUIZ

1. Is the smaller boat to the **LEFT** or **RIGHT** of the big ship?

2. Are the flowers **INSIDE** or **OUTSIDE** the flower shop?

3. Is the child **ON** or **OFF** the scooter?

The answers can be found on page 30.

WHAT AM I QUIZ

1. I am BEHIND the bus. What am I?

2. I am in FRONT of a skyscraper. What am I?

3. I am UNDER an umbrella. What am I?

The answers can be found on page 31.

WHERE IS IT QUIZ ANSWERS

1. The small boat is on the **LEFT** side of the big ship.

2. The flowers are **OUTSIDE** the shop.

3. The child is **ON** the scooter.

WHAT AM I QUIZ ANSWERS

1. I am **BEHIND** the bus. I am a car.

2. I am in **FRONT** of a skyscraper. I am a tree.

3. I am **UNDER** the umbrella. I am a dog.

LOOK FOR THE OTHER BOOKS IN THE WORLD AROUND YOU SERIES!

AUTHOR BIO

Christianne Jones has read about a bazillion books, written more than 70, and edited about 1,000. Christianne works as a book editor and lives in Mankato, Minnesota, with her husband and three daughters.